DISCARD

W9-AEY-805

MAR   2008

Markham Public Libraries
Milliken Mills Library
7600 Kennedy Road, Unit 1
Markham, ON L3R 9S5

JENNIFER LOPEZ

by
Jill C. Wheeler

Visit us at
www.abdopub.com

Published by ABDO Publishing Company, 4940 Viking Drive, Edina, MN 55435. Copyright ©2003 by Abdo Consulting Group, Inc. International copyrights reserved in all countries. No part of this book may be reproduced in any form without written permission from the publisher.

Printed in the United States.

Graphic Design: John Hamilton
Cover Design: MacLean Tuminelly
Cover photo: Corbis
Interior photos:
   AP/Wide World, p. 1, 7, 9, 10, 39, 43, 53, 59, 62
   Corbis, p. 5, 12-13, 15, 17, 18, 21, 22, 24-25, 27, 29, 31, 35, 36, 40, 45, 47, 49, 51, 55, 57, 60-61

Library of Congress Cataloging-in-Publication Data

Wheeler, Jill C., 1964-
   Jennifer Lopez / Jill C. Wheeler.
      p. cm. — (Star tracks)
   Includes index.
   Summary: A biography of Jennifer Lopez, whose talent and determination have led to her success as an actress, singer, and dancer.
ISBN 1-57765-770-5
      1. Lopez, Jennifer, 1970—Juvenile literature.
2. Singers—United States—Biography—Juvenile literature.
[1. Lopez, Jennifer, 1970- 2. Actors and actresses.
3. Singers. 4. Women—Biography. 5. Hispanic Americans.]
I. Title. II. Series.

ML3930.L66 W44 2002
791.43'028'092—dc21
[B]
                                        2002018360

CONTENTS

AMERICA
GOES

L A T I N

IN THE SUMMER OF 1999, A YOUNG PUERTO Rican singer named Ricky Martin burst onto the pop music scene. It was hard to watch the television or scan magazine racks without seeing at least one image of the handsome singer. His single "Livin' la Vida Loca" (Livin' the Crazy Life) rocketed to the top of the pop charts within days of its release. Suddenly, people across America were craving the Latin sound.

Latinos have been a part of the American entertainment scene for years. However, they often perform in Spanish, so their audiences are limited to Spanish-speaking people. Martin was among the first to make traditional Latino rhythms and musical styles a hit with a broader audience.

Many people in the entertainment industry believe Martin's success paved the way for other Latino performers to broaden their appeal. In fact, it was a single by another Latino artist that finally bumped "Livin' la Vida Loca" from the top of the charts. The single was the first song ever released by Jennifer Lopez. And unlike Martin, who had cut his entertainment teeth in the popular boy band Menudo, she had never recorded before. Lopez had, however, already turned heads in Hollywood.

Jennifer credits her success not only to talent, but also to hard work.

By the time her single "If You Had My Love" pushed "Livin' la Vida Loca" from the number one spot, Lopez had millions of fans. She was an accomplished dancer, and the highest-paid Latina actress in history.

Lopez credits her success not only to talent but to hard work as well. In fact, she thrives on it. "I get my work ethic from my parents," she said. "I feel like I haven't even started yet. I'm looking forward to the ninth album, the thirtieth movie. I want to write more songs, tour, find the right roles, have my own family. That's why I have so much energy. I know what lies ahead."

"I just know what I was born to do," she said. "I have one of those brains. I'm dreaming about what I'm going to do before I wake up."

BRONX BEAUTY

JENNIFER LOPEZ WAS BORN ON JULY 24, 1970, in the Castle Hill section of the Bronx. The Bronx is one of New York City's boroughs. Jennifer's parents were David and Guadalupe Lopez, both of whom had been born in Puerto Rico. They moved to the United States as children and later met in the Bronx. David worked nights as a computer technician for an insurance company. Guadalupe, or Lupe as she is known, taught kindergarten at the Holy Family Catholic School.

Growing up in the Bronx was not always easy. It was one of New York City's poorer neighborhoods. There were gangs in the area, and many families struggled to get by. Jennifer recalls her family's apartment being cold in the winter and hot in the summer. Yet the Lopez family lived well by local standards.

Jennifer's parents passed on their love of music to her.

Jennifer, her older sister Leslie, and younger sister Lynda, quickly learned that hard work was important. "Our parents had a strong work ethic," recalled Lynda. "There wasn't really any other way. They led by example. They would tell us we could never miss a day of work—and they didn't. They told us we had to go to church every week, which they did. They never had any downtime. I didn't realize people were any different until I was a teenager."

Jennifer's parents also passed a love of music on to their daughters. David often sang, and Lupe usually had some kind of music playing. "My mom would play a lot of music," Jennifer said. "Mostly things from her childhood; doo-wop, the Shirelles, the Ronettes, the Supremes." Every Sunday, Lupe would tape Casey Kasem's *American Top 40* countdown on the radio. Then she'd listen to the songs again while cleaning the house. Lupe also enjoyed musicals and at one time had dreamed of being a singer and actress.

Singing and dancing seemed to come naturally to Jennifer. She remembers dancing on the family table as a toddler. As a young girl, she began taking singing and dancing lessons. Early on, she knew exactly what she wanted to be when she grew up. "The kind of career I always aspired to was very much from the musicals I used to watch when I was young," Jennifer recalls.

ANYTHING
FOR
APPLAUSE

LIKE MANY YOUNG LATINOS IN THE UNITED States, Jennifer's world was a mix of cultures. "It's funny, as you grow up in this country, you don't think about it but you're influenced by everything," she said. "I listened to salsa and merengue, but I also listened to Cher."

One of Jennifer's early influences was the movie *West Side Story*. It is a musical retelling of Shakespeare's play *Romeo & Juliet*. In the play, two young lovers want to be together even though their families disapprove of their relationship. In *West Side Story*, the characters are Puerto Rican and the story takes place in New York City.

"I've seen it more than 100 times," Jennifer said of *West Side Story*. "I loved that it was a musical about Puerto Ricans and that they were living were I lived." Jennifer often dreamed of acting in *West Side Story* when she grew up. As a child, she and her sisters would put on shows in the family living room and act out scenes from the musical. "Jennifer was always Anita, the fiery one," her father said. Jennifer said about her earliest performances, "We used to do little shows, even if it was just cartwheels. Whatever made them clap, we did."

"She always loved to sing, but she was also a born actress," said Lupe. "Ever since she was a little girl she was acting, living in her own world."

Jennifer and her sisters attended Catholic school for 12 years, including an all-girls Catholic high school. Her lessons expanded to include piano and acting. A tomboy and natural athlete, Jennifer also participated in tennis, softball, gymnastics, and went out for track. "I recall asking why she was going out for track," her father said. "I thought she'd get outclassed, because she'd never done anything like that. If she starts something, all that happens is she gets better." He was absolutely right. Jennifer ended up competing nationally in track.

Jennifer recalls that her life changed in her mid-teens. "That was the start of the boyfriend years," she said. "It was all about the house and family until I was 16; then I fell in love, and it was all about sneaking away from the house and family." Jennifer had a long-time boyfriend named David Cruz. However, her family didn't approve of them dating. For Jennifer, it was like a scene out of *West Side Story*. "I was always climbing out windows, jumping off roofs, and he was sneaking up," she said. "It was crazy."

Jennifer signed autographs August 17, 2000, at the Los Angeles premiere of The Cell.

Jennifer also started her professional acting career at age 16. She and her sister Lynda had performed in local musical theater groups and in high school plays. In 1986, Jennifer landed a bit part in a movie called *My Little Girl*. Her sister also landed a part in a movie, but decided later not to pursue the acting life. "She has a great voice and had more of a chance of making it than I did, but she couldn't take the rejection," Jennifer said. Today, Lynda is a VJ on VH1 and a DJ at a New York radio station. Their older sister Leslie is a music teacher.

"All three of my daughters have talent," said David Lopez. "Jennifer is the one with the drive to put it all together. She's in a tough world, but you've got to realize who the person is. She was always very competitive."

Jennifer started her professional acting career at age 16.

DANCING
DAYS

FOLLOWING HIGH SCHOOL, LOPEZ HAD A tough decision to make. She knew her parents wanted her to go to college and then to law school. But she wanted a career in the entertainment industry.

"They [her parents] wanted me to be a lawyer," Lopez said. "Actually, I think I would have been an OK lawyer. I don't think I would have been a very happy lawyer. I would be in front of the jury, singing."

At Preston High School, Lopez had earned a reputation as a talented dancer and choreographer. After graduation in 1987, she decided to study dance at Baruch College in New York. But she dropped out after one semester. She then took a job in a law office and spent her spare time at dance classes and auditions. At night she danced in clubs, performing pieces her dance teacher had choreographed. Meanwhile her parents were very concerned about their daughter spending so much time in nightclubs.

Jennifer's mother once told her, "You wanted to be in this business, so you better toughen up."

"I lived at home until my mom and I came at odds about me doing this for a living," Lopez said. "She was worried about me. I was 18; I worked in Manhattan and would then hang out at this dance studio and clubs. I really would just go into the club and go right out. I never drank, but she didn't know that. She worried about me getting mixed up with the wrong people."

About that time, musical artist M.C. Hammer had hit it big with "U Can't Touch This," and the new sound in music was hip-hop. "All the auditions started becoming hip-hop auditions," Lopez recalls. "I was good at it, and they were like, 'Ooh, a light-skinned girl who can do that. Great, let's hire her!'"

Lopez took a string of low-paying hip-hop gigs just to get by. Then she landed a five-month job dancing in the European tour of *Golden Musicals of Broadway*. She recalls learning a hard lesson while on tour when she was the only dancer who didn't get a solo. "I called up my mom crying because I didn't think I'd been given a fair shake," she said. "I thought she'd offer me some sympathy. Instead she said, 'Don't you ever call me crying again! You wanted to be in this business, so you better toughen up.'"

Lopez did toughen up, and she went on to do a Japanese tour of another theater production, *Synchronicity*, as well as dance in a number of music videos.

A lifelong New Yorker, Lopez had always hoped to dance on Broadway. But she finally realized there were greater opportunities for her in Hollywood. In 1991, one of those opportunities presented itself.

FLY
GIRL

LOPEZ KNEW ENOUGH ABOUT SHOW business to know that she had to find high-profile gigs. She went on many auditions in her early years. Yet the one that gave her career the necessary break was for a new television comedy called *In Living Color*. Lopez was one of more than 2,000 young women vying for a job as one of the show's Fly Girl dancers. The Fly Girls performed hip-hop routines between comedy sketches.

Despite the competition, Lopez landed the job. It wasn't exactly what she wanted—she would rather have landed an acting job. Yet she knew she could use the high-profile part for her next move. She made sure the show's producer, Keenan Ivory Wayans, knew that she really wanted to act. He advised her to do *In Living Color* for two seasons and then look for something else. His advice proved to be right on the mark.

In Living Color exposed Lopez to many influential people. Her choreographer was Rosie Perez, who went on to her own acting career. Lopez impressed many of the people she met. "There was just an unshakable confidence about Jennifer," recalled the co-producer of the show. "No doubt, no fear. The girl just had it."

The show also meant Lopez had to move to Los Angeles. "*In Living Color* was nice because it was my first steady paycheck," Lopez remembers. "But I was miserable living in L.A. I'm a total New York-Bronx girl, with the accent and the whole nine. I was hating it. It's a really lonely city when you're an East Coast person. But now I love L.A."

Lopez spent most of her money the first year flying back home on weekends. Later, her boyfriend, David Cruz, joined her in L.A. "He wound up staying out there for four years with me," Lopez said. "I was stable at home, so I was able to excel and work."

And work she did. After two years on *In Living Color*, she was offered a part in a new FOX television series called *South Central*. Lopez played a clerk in a co-op market on the short-lived series. Her part was small, but she captured people's attention. The role helped her land a job in the television series *Second Chances*.

Second Chances aired for only one season.
Still, Lopez's character, Melinda Lopez, was very
popular. Her character appeared in a spin-off series
called *Malibu Road*. It too failed in the television
ratings game. However, the exposure helped land
Lopez several other television roles, including
Nurses on the Line: The Crash of Flight 7.

"I was stable at home, so I was able to excel and work."

ON TO THE
BIG
SCREEN

FROM TELEVISION, LOPEZ MOVED ON TO work in feature films. Her first was *My Family/Mi Familia*. *My Family/Mi Familia* was an art film with a small budget. The 1995 film told the story of three generations of a Mexican family that immigrated to California in the 1920s. Lopez acted alongside accomplished actors Edward James Olmos and Jimmy Smits.

Director Gregory Nava was impressed with Jennifer's abilities, as well as her dedication. In the movie Lopez's character, Maria Sanchez, is de-

JIMMY SMITS · ESAI MORALES · EDWARD JAMES OLMOS

MY FAMILY

Three generations of dreams.

"*My Family* is ambitious and sweeping!
A generational epic like *The Godfather.*"
—Roger Ebert, Chicago Sun-Times

ported to Mexico and must fight her way back to her husband and children in California. At one point she has to cross a frigid river. "She got right into that freezing water every day for three days and came through without ever complaining," recalls Nava. "Few actresses would be that heroic and courageous. She's going to be a big star," he predicted.

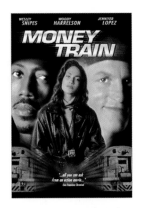

Lopez's next role was in the 1995 action film *Money Train*. The film is about two New York City transit cops who decide to rob the train that gathers the money collected at the city's subway stations. Lopez played an undercover police officer who was also the romantic interest of the two main characters, played by Wesley Snipes and Woody Harrelson.

Before doing *Money Train*, Lopez did her homework. She talked with police officers, especially female officers, to get a feel for what it was like to do that job. She wanted to find out how female officers were treated by their male colleagues.

Critics didn't care much for *Money Train*. Fortunately for Lopez, that didn't reflect badly on her. In fact, her next part was in a movie directed by film legend Francis Ford Coppola. Coppola had seen her performance in *My Family/Mi Familia* and wanted her to audition for his new movie, *Jack*.

Jack is the story of a boy with a disease that makes him grow four times faster than normal. The boy, played by Robin Williams, looks 40 years old when he's only 10. In the film, he attends school outside his home for the first time in fifth grade. He develops a crush on his teacher, played by Lopez.

Lopez enjoyed playing a teacher, and she enjoyed working with Williams and Coppola. She also was pleased that her role was not originally written as a Latina part. While Lopez is proud of her heritage, she regards herself as an actress first and a Latina second. She doesn't believe that her ethnic background should limit or define her roles.

Jack

HARD-WORKING

A C T R E S S

BY 1997, LOPEZ HAD APPEARED IN THREE feature films. That same year, she appeared in four more. In the thriller *Blood and Wine*, Lopez played the Cuban mistress of Jack Nicholson. One of their first scenes together included a salsa dance. While Lopez was intimidated working with legendary actor Nicholson, she taught him a few dance steps. That helped to ease some of her tension.

In the action-adventure film *Anaconda*, Lopez played a film director. In the movie, she and her crew plan to do a documentary on a native tribe in the jungles of South America. Instead, they end up fighting a 40-foot (12-meter)-long snake. The role took Lopez to the Amazon basin near Manaus, Brazil for filming, and she found it hard to be that far from home. Yet she enjoyed the challenge of doing an action film. She also enjoyed playing a strong female character.

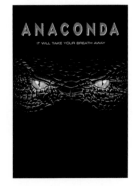

"I always made the choice to do different things."

Lopez marked another milestone in her career with her appearance in the film *U-Turn*. Oliver Stone directed the movie, and it offered Lopez the chance to work with more Hollywood greats, including Nick Nolte, Sean Penn, and Billy Bob Thornton. Once again, it was a role not determined by ethnicity. Lopez is proud that she's made the choices she has, even though they weren't always the obvious ones.

"I always made the choice to do different things," she said. "I took the other role, the one that in the long run would mean more, even if it wasn't the one that might have put more money in the bank."

Lopez might not have known it at the time, but she was about to take a role that would put money in the bank and her career on the road to superstardom.

SELENA

IN 1995, MUSIC FANS WERE SHOCKED BY the murder of Tejano superstar Selena Quintanilla Perez. The 23-year-old singer was gunned down by the president of her own fan club. It happened just after Selena had recorded her first English-language album and had won a Grammy Award.

The Hispanic community reeled at the news of Selena's death. She had become a folk hero to them. She was a woman from humble beginnings who had made it big despite the odds. It wasn't long before talk turned to making a movie of her life. Gregory Nava, the same man who directed *My Family/Mi Familia*, would direct it.

Nava knew whoever played the part of Selena would have a tough job. Selena's many fans would be very critical of the film. Whoever starred as their slain hero would need to put her own feelings aside and play Selena as close to the original as possible.

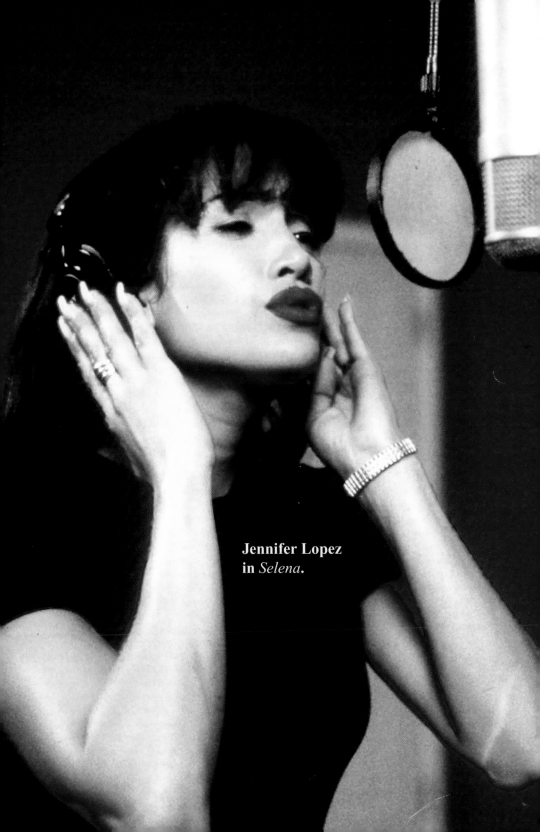

Jennifer Lopez
in *Selena*.

Jennifer was a natural for the part of Selena.

Nava held open casting calls for the part, and some 22,000 young women tried out. One of them was Jennifer Lopez. Nava already knew she could act. But it took Lopez several auditions to convince him that she was up for the challenge. "Not only did Jennifer give the best audition," said Nava, "we were looking for someone who could capture Selena's inner spirit. She just had it."

When Lopez signed her $1 million contract for the movie, she became the highest-paid Latina actress ever. Once again she did her homework for the part. She studied Selena's dancing and gestures, and even spent time with Selena's family.

Lopez was a natural for the part. With just a little makeup, she looked like Selena's twin. Soon she danced the same way. The Quintanilla family insisted that Lopez lip-synch the singing scenes so Selena's real voice could be played in the movie. But Lopez still got the thrill of performing in front of a roaring crowd. It got her thinking about singing for herself.

"I've almost forgotten how much I like to perform onstage because I've been caught up in doing films," she said. "It was great getting in front of an audience, getting that immediate response… I liked it! And that week I told my managers I wanted to record something. I've gotta record an album. I love doing it so much."

In Lopez's personal life, 1997 also was a special year. In March of the previous year, her boyfriend David Cruz had moved back to New York. Lopez claims her success had taken its toll on their relationship, and they agreed it was best to end it. While filming *Blood and Wine*, she had met a Cuban waiter named Ojani Noa, and they began dating. At the party following the end of filming *Selena,* Noa proposed to her, and she accepted. The two married in February 1997.

The marriage lasted just a year, and Jennifer cites her youth and her career as primary causes for its end. "I was young and naive and thought that love conquered the world," she said. "But you have to compromise to a certain extent. [Success] changes things… "

Jennifer Lopez and former husband Ojani Noa arrive at the premiere of Anaconda *in Los Angeles, April 7, 1997.*

CROSSOVER STAR

SELENA EARNED LOPEZ A GOLDEN GLOBE nomination, along with more respect in the film community. She used her success to seek the female lead in the 1998 movie *Out of Sight*. George Clooney had already been signed to play the male lead, a prison escapee. Lopez wanted to play the federal marshal with whom he has a romance.

Clooney insisted on a screen test with anyone who wanted the role. He wanted to make sure they had the right chemistry together. Sandra Bullock, who had been considered for the role, refused. Lopez agreed, and she and Clooney sizzled on screen. Lopez earned $2 million for her work. This broke her own Hollywood record for the highest salary of a Latina actress.

In 1998, Lopez also began putting her voice to work. She was the voice of one of the characters in the 1998 computer-animated film *Antz*. Then she took a year off from movies to follow another dream.

As a child, Lopez had longed to combine singing and acting. Doing *Selena* reminded her of how much she enjoyed singing. Now she was ready to take her career in a different direction. She wanted to record a pop album. She had a number of professional musician friends to help her. They included Miami Sound Machine's Emilio Estefan, Latin singer Marc Antony, and rapper Sean "Puff Daddy" Combs.

In June 1999, Lopez released *On the 6*. She named the CD after the train she used to ride from the Bronx into Manhattan for auditions. Lopez called the music "Latin soul." It combined elements of traditional Latin music with hip-hop and rhythm and blues. Her first single, "If You Had My Love," became the number-one single on *Billboard*

magazine's Hot 100 chart.

On the 6 went double platinum. The video of the single "If You Had My Love" was also a huge success, offering Lopez's fans a chance to see her cool dance moves again.

Combs had produced one of Lopez's songs for *On the 6*. And while Lopez said he was just a friend, the rumors said otherwise. Eventually, the two admitted they were dating. They had a lot in common. Both came from humble beginnings and had worked hard to make it big. Both also wanted to make it even bigger.

Lopez and Combs dated for two years. Their often stormy relationship made many headlines in the gossip tabloids. The headlines peaked in December 1999 when the two were arrested following a shooting at a New York City nightclub. Lopez was held by the police for questioning for 14 hours. At one point, she was even handcuffed to a bench in the police station. Eventually she was released and charges against her were dropped.

In February 2000, Lopez and Combs created a louder buzz at the Grammy Awards. Both had been nominated for awards, Lopez for *On the 6*. She wore a revealing dress to the awards ceremony. Some people claimed she only did it for attention. Lopez disagreed. "I wore it because it was just a nice dress," she said. Shortly after the awards, the couple went their separate ways.

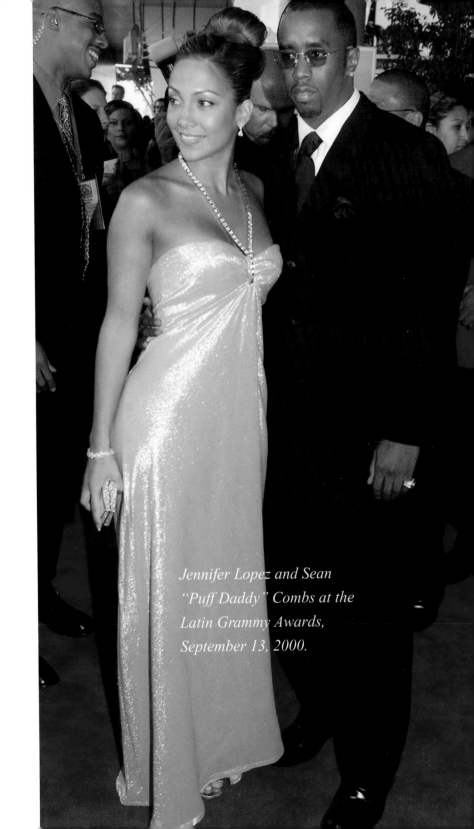

*Jennifer Lopez and Sean
"Puff Daddy" Combs at the
Latin Grammy Awards,
September 13, 2000.*

BACK
ON THE
SET

LOPEZ RETURNED TO MAKING MOVIES after her success with *On the 6*. She shot three movies back-to-back. In *The Cell* she played a child therapist who helps the Federal Bureau of Investigation catch a serial killer. In *Angel Eyes* she again played a police officer, this one intrigued by a drifter. In *The Wedding Planner* she was a very organized, professional wedding planner. Her character ends up falling in love with the man her client is going to marry.

Amazingly, Lopez had time to work on a new album while doing the movies. She released her second album, *J. Lo*, in early 2001. Lopez wrote four of the album's songs. Critics said it was even better than *On the 6*. The album sold more than 272,000 copies in the first week. It rocketed to the top of *Billboard* magazine's Top 200 chart, edging out a Beatles greatest hits album.

While *J. Lo* was making headlines, *The Wedding Planner* was stealing the show. It grossed $14 million in its first weekend, making it the top movie in North America at the time. Combined, the two blockbusters made Lopez the only entertainer to have the top-grossing movie and the number one non-soundtrack album in the same week.

Vince Vaughn, director of *The Cell,* said, "Jennifer is one of those people who prove that the more you do, the more you can do. On the set, she never seemed stressed. She has so much energy and willpower; she's a force of nature. But she's able to focus it and use it productively." Her hairdresser added, "She's the hardest-working person I know."

Lopez turned her focus to more personal matters in 2001. The year before, she had met a young dancer named Cris Judd. Judd had performed in Lopez's video "Love Don't Cost a Thing." He also helped choreograph two of her concerts that summer. In August 2001, Lopez and Judd announced they were engaged.

On September 29, 2001, Lopez and Judd were married in a small ceremony in Calabasas, California. Following the ceremony, they honeymooned in Italy.

Those close to Lopez say Judd is very different from the flamboyant Combs. They also say he seems to be a better match for her and a calming influence in her hectic life. Lopez agrees. "He's wonderful," she said. "He is very understanding."

Jennifer Lopez and Cris Judd at their September 29, 2001, wedding.

DIVA

LOPEZ'S SUCCESS HAS BROUGHT WITH IT
some controversy. Early in her career, she said
unkind things about entertainers Madonna,
Cameron Diaz, Winona Ryder, and Gwyneth
Paltrow in a magazine interview. Reportedly, she
later sent notes of apology to them. Rumors also
swirl that Lopez has a big ego and can be very
demanding.

People who work with Lopez say the stories
are exaggerated. "A lot of times, when people,
especially women, attain a certain status—when
they raise their hand and say 'I want it,' with no
guilt—they get that title, diva, put on them," said
director Vaughn. "I only deal with people how they
deal with me, and never did I see Jennifer take
advantage of her position, or belittle or bully
anyone. I think she's handling everything with a lot
of grace."

Throughout her career, Lopez has also had to defend her body type. Some have criticized her for being fuller figured than most Hollywood actresses. Lopez says she won't change and that she's comfortable with her body just the way it is.

"When I first got into the business, people were like, 'Oh, you need to be thinner,'" she said. "It made me self-conscious for a minute. Then I was like, Why do I have to live up to the ideal of someone else? Everyone doesn't have the same exact body. That's so ridiculous."

No one can deny the 5-foot 6-inch tall actress is a beauty. *People* magazine has included her on its 50 Most Beautiful People list several times. L'Oréal cosmetics signed her up as a spokeswoman. And while she refuses to fit the wafer-thin stereotype of Hollywood, Lopez enjoys being physically fit. She runs and lifts weights to stay in shape.

Recently, Lopez took up the martial art Krav Maga (krahv muh-GAH). Krav Maga is a defense system taught to the Israeli armed forces. She began studying Krav Maga to prepare for her role in the new movie *Enough*. In *Enough*, Lopez plays an abused wife who decides to fight back against her abuser.

Jennifer Lopez shows off her award for Best Dance Video at the MTV Video Music Awards in New York, September 7, 2000.

J. LO
INCORPORATED

ONE OF LOPEZ'S LATEST PROJECTS IS A new line of clothing called J. Lo. The designs are inspired by her own unique look. They include hip-hugger jeans, cropped tops, and athletic wear. They're also designed to fit a variety of body types. "I wanted to offer clothes that are wonderfully designed and fit women of all sizes," Lopez explained.

For her next projects, Lopez is looking at several movies, including a movie about the life of Mexican artist Frida Kahlo. Lopez's work has already opened doors for other Latina entertainers, and she wants to continue to do that. She's considering a modern version of the classic opera *Carmen*, complete with flamenco dancing. Or there's always that remake of *West Side Story*. "I'd play Maria," she said.

Then, in true Jennifer Lopez fashion she added, "But I'd have to play Anita, too... "

Jennifer Lopez smiles in front of a giant poster of herself during a welcome ceremony at a Hong Kong hotel February 19, 2001. She was in Hong Kong for a three-day promotional tour.

Jennifer Lopez performed in San Juan, Puerto Rico, September 22, 2001.

GLOSSARY

borough: a self-governing, basic unit of local government. There are five boroughs, or subdivisions, in New York City.

doo-wop: a style of pop music that was popular in the 1950s. Doo-wop features a lead singer supported by a chorus. It often has instruments with a strong, rhythmic beat.

flamenco: a style of song and dance that originated in southern Spain. Flamenco dancing is characterized by stamping and clapping. The music is usually very emotional and mournful.

merengue: a type of Latin American dance music. Merengue, which originated in the Dominican Republic in the nineteenth century, is a fast ballroom dance in which dancers keep one leg stiff.

WEB SITES

Would you like to learn more about Jennifer Lopez? Please visit **www.abdopub.com** to find up-to-date Web site links about Jennifer Lopez, her music, and acting career. These links are routinely monitored and updated to provide the most current information available.

INDEX

Markham Public Libraries
Milliken Mills Library
7600 Kennedy Road, Unit 1
Markham, ON L3R 9S5